Burnt Lavender

John Queor

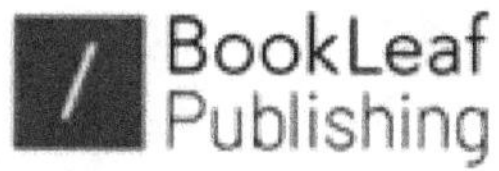

BookLeaf Publishing

Presentation by *BookLeaf Publishing*

Web: www.bookleafpub.com

E-mail: info@bookleafpub.com

ISBN : 9789357210201

First edition 2022

DEDICATION

To Norma, who always encourages me to be seen.

Initium

The cosmos cracked their iron gate
And I began my first great plummet
Surrounded by blackness until blue
Where I found myself in an ocean
Floating free with peace radiating
Pure essence with a hint of longing
To begin the journey of becoming
A being with wisdom and battle scars
To ascend and descend a billion times
Harboring glimpses of other lives
And seeing faces that once were mine
The water began to softly ripple
When soon a vortex emerged beside me
And I allowed the current to pull me down
And pull me down, and pull me down...

Sprout

A golden hue was everywhere
Warmth sweetly caressed my skin
As I galloped on the plush grass
Cooing, screaming, giggling
My hair was angelic white
My eyes were the ocean

My roots weren't tethered deep
A gust of wind could have stolen me
But they were imbedded in the dirt
And watered when it was necessary

A golden hue was everywhere
Spring days became summer nights
And as time spun I hastily grew
The connection was always stressed
As my roots never plunged any further
And I wondered if I would ever bloom

Blackout

One evening the sun went down
And forgot to come back up
For years I existed in only night
Unable to gaze upon my reflection
Until my eyes had finally acclimated
And then I had no idea what I was seeing
Other than recognizing a silhouette
Resembling the haze of a shadow
Mimicking the moves I was making

Maybe the star I was wishing on
Was just a distant satellite twinkling
My discussions were one sided
Usually slurred and unheard

One evening in that darkness
A memory of light had emerged
Enough so to create a spark
And I spit out my gasoline
Which ignited a small fire
And once my hands were warm
I lit my entire body aflame
To become that distant star
That I had put such faith in

Husk

I periodically
Throw funerals for myself
Quite simple
Closed casket quick eulogy
Fresh lavender
I never use roses as goodbyes
Mourn momentarily
The piece I'm giving up
Always growing
But trying not to collect
Particles obsolete
Like smoking cigarettes
Lonesome alcoholism
Trying to speed up the end
Missing moments
Like sitting in the quiet
Sipping lemon balm
Planning another burial
Perhaps cremation
We are ever changing
Forever discarding
Old skin and malignant habits

Rise

5

It had been quite a while
Since I'd seen
The stars overthrown
By the bursting oil spill
Of the climbing sun
It once was
A reoccurring routine
To watch the light
Fill the cracks
Of the curtains
Before sleeping
Better yet
Passing out
Actually
Letting go
Finally
Drifting off
In a sea of sad
And empty
Bottles
To soon after
Repeat

Satyr

Honeysuckle lips far away somewhere
I can no longer reach even in my sleep
But for one night you sweetly did reside
In the neurons vibrating behind my eyes
In a pastel scene gleaming golden pristine
A sunset on grass unimaginably green

Honey brown eyes sweet and bright
You were the only star I recall that night
A kiss so gentle it brought me to tears
Taming my pain and hushing my fears
Skin alabaster under the moonshine
That wondrous night that you were mine

Honey bees could never leave such a sting
As waking in bright sunlight without you
And when I rise from tonight's dreaming
The fate's will have had their fun scheming
For more details will have dissipated
My hopes of returning surely eliminated

Cleanse

I hung a branch of eucalyptus
From my shower head
So that I may heal faster
When my mind transforms
Into Judas or Brute

Visualizing each one of my
Dark and intrusive thoughts
Slipping into the vortex
To swirl down the drain

Healing is much more than
Stitches and medication
It's a battle and decision
To always find the light
Even when the moon is new

Constellation kaleidoscope

It all seems so black and white
The nothingness scattered
With clusters of sedimentary orbs
That map out why you are
The way you are
Until you decide to hone in
And the colors emerge
Baby blues and blushing orange
The grey of receding shadows
Whispers of burnt rose
Wisps of yellow haze
Kisses of ultraviolet
And all of a sudden
Things begin to change
As the realization hits
That nothing has ever been
Just black or white
Your eyes simply couldn't see
The colors hidden deep
In the endless gasses burning

Highway

Vapors rushing out from the open windows
Going too quickly down a side street
With bass exploding around us cruising
White knuckle fists in my lap balled
Shrieking as you dodge and swerve
Then laughing through the anxiety of
Surviving riding with a street pirate
Who wishes to explore other avenues
Beyond the quaint city we grew up in
And I forget that people can be discontent
With the continuity of constant comfort
I'm a bull who can lull on pastel clouds
He is ruled by water and wants to sail
There's excitement to be found in chaos
But who can tell which role I'll play
Arachnid or small fly buzzing trapped
I guess to gamble is the point
And everything will one day be memory
Swiftly changing lanes and accelerating
Like my brother on the highway

Linear

These fallen grains of sand pack a punch
Clusters of people and places that once
Meant everything to me are boiled down
To a syrup sticky not meant to ingest

Bookmarks and landmarks and old hearts
That I really don't know or recognize anymore

Sometimes a scent or sensation or sky color
Drags me back to years I forgot were forgotten
And we were so confident in never forgetting
Lines will soon dance on our eyes and smiles

Desensitizing isn't the armor I hoped for
It's like saving the whipped cream for last

Pools and puddles and oceans of time
Getting ahead leaves me behind
Because nothing is really linear
It's just there until it's not there

Burnt Lavender

Bustling north wind whistling
Under dim lit stars twinkling
Returning to the inner void
Numbing the joyous feeling
Tethering me to tranquility

Lingering feelings within
Alignment to the angry tides
Vexing undertow grasping
Entangling it's cold fingers
Navigating up and around
Denying true freedom
Except when enveloped in
Rising billows of burnt lavender

Downstream

Chaos once convinced me
Swimming upstream was necessary
To be my absolute most authentic self
Simplicity seemed like surrendering
And in a sense it truly was

Just before I almost drowned
I let the water guide me
I drifted gently down
Around soft curvatures
Experiencing the banks

Finally after some time
I found myself floating still
Inhaling full lunged breaths
And exhaling soft and slow
With my eyes completely closed

And I surrendered
I let simplicity take me
Down a whole new avenue
Of being who I am
And fully enjoying it

Star talk

My conversations with the cosmos
Have become a welcomed nightly ritual
And although there is little rebuttal
There are noticeable changes occuring

Despite urges to request a multitude
Of mundane objects and blessings
I find peace in expressing gratitude
For everything this life has allowed me

My conversations with the cosmos
Are not extremely clear and concise
My mind is not always cheery and bright
But I am grateful for our nightly exchange

Along with the comfort of change
Happening within and around me

Transfer

There is no ebb and flow
Found in the sea of stars
Just continuous light
Until one must explode
And they let it go
To transfer elsewhere
As a firefly or
Intricate snowflake
To land and melt
And transfer elsewhere
As a bluebird or
Small acorn
To seed and sprout
Reach for the clouds
Live peacefully mostly
Uninterrupted except for
Birds making shelter
Children climbing limbs
Until men encroach
To introduce their axes
Turning it into furniture
Ensuing another transfer
To become a carpenter

Anima

Another milestone approached
A park bench in a familiar place
Tucked deeply in the subconscious
Where I sometimes visit when I sleep
Surrounded by infinite shards of light
Peeking from behind the curtains

My church is a small gazebo
Hidden deeply in the lush filigree
Tucked safely behind my eyes
When I'm calm enough to travel
And brave enough to go inside
Where my essence does reside

Radiating light and high vibration
Decorated in lavender and baby's breath
I gazed in a silver basin and asked respectfully
Whether or not I had changed enough
My reflection returned strong and clear
No longer a hazy shadow apparition

Visit

Moments kept safe in an old cigar box
Locked securely in my cranial attic
That I climb up to when I need some quiet
From a world that has been burning for eons
I lock the door behind me and breathe
Inviting an influx of images to overwhelm me

Crashing tides of the cool blue ocean
Snow covered train tracks late evening
Stargazing cocooned in a sleeping bag
A circle in the woods behind my house
A bicycle track my dad hand plowed
The fallen trees that formed a fortress
The standing tree that cradled me
Jumping from the ledge at little falls
Haphazard afternoon car rides stoned
Seneca smoke rising to the starlight
Sitting atop the green bridge laughing
Midnight walks down lampless streets
My aunt's front porch where I would write
The quiet pond at grandpa's camp
Sleeping in grandma's pink apartment
Blowing bubbles from the balcony
Running from the mothman with Allie
Making clouds of smoke behind the mall
Learning how to make an Alabama Slammer

A first kiss beneath the purple sky
Schnapps in a water bottle downtown
Coming home from the B2 in Squeaky
Dancing with strangers in flashing lights
Intense conversations at sunrise

I could spend forever in the attic
With a hot cup of lavender honey tea
But it's not good to spend too much time
Waltzing with ghosts far departed
The present has been beyond kind
But I sometimes stop back for a visit

Oasis

I'm content to stay perched
Amongst the clouds meandering
By my south facing windows
But once in a while I'm contacted
With requests to venture below
To create new experiences

I love to watch the machine work
As I sit on my balcony at night
Electricity creating star mimicry
And I feel like I'm in heaven

I create an oasis around me
So that it might mirror inside
On days that are darker
Harder to navigate through

I'm content to stay strewn
Sprawled on soft surfaces
Letting the sun come and go
Watching the moon drift on
By the wide open window
As I relish in sweet solitude

Luminaria

I am a mosaic of small incredible moments
So many people make up the pieces of me
Glossy stained glass in a grand cathedral
Creating an abstract scene of Nirvana

I am thankful for each situation
And all the hands I've held thus far
Guiding me along this winding venture
And I hope that others feel the same
We may each be one spec of light
But with kindness we enhance our glow
And create an example to pass on
For those who may feel low

We are all mosaics of small miracles
Every one of us a shooting star
Cruising through the darkness
With help from each others light

Placement

It gets so monotonous being amongst
A billion blades of grass competing
For the searing lust of the sun
I want to bide my time and disintegrate
Sink deep into the soft blanket soil

Find myself finally totally floating free
Beyond the dark side of the moon
Wearing constellations as a crown
And a black hole as a necklace
Utilizing a nebula as a pillow
To recline watching meteor storms

Silver shimmers of solar showers
Slip into dreams of past lives
Focusing on perfecting balance
Waiting for the divine to decide
How I performed on the placement
And as the right planets align
Place me somewhere appropriate

Soul Flowers

I gift to gravity all that weighs me down
Freeing my hands to hold what enhances
Allowing my shoulders to sit a bit higher
To deeply breathe and find my center
Exhaling what no longer serves me

I allow the stagnant toxins to ooze
Creep from my bones into the earth
To seed and grow into wild flowers
Littering the stone path behind me
For others to discover on their way

And perhaps I'll read a poem one day
By a healing soul describing their beauty
Because I never looked back
Because I no longer needed to
Because the gifts I gave to gravity

Home

Soul ascending back into cosmic kisses
Aurora Borealis' open bright arms
First aid kit nestled deep in the stars
To fix these gnarly earthly wounds

I was never really interested in aviation
Touching the sky wouldn't bring me home
Where beyond the atmosphere did hide
A door accessible for me when I was ready

Soul ascending in iridescent sunbeams
Warmth caressing my face and hair
Gravity once again takes another gift and
Allows me a moment of pure reflection

I was never really interested in longevity
Homesick from the moment I got here
For a home I could no longer remember
But longed for so strongly in my core

Soul ascending like a fireworks finale
One last goodbye to my lives here
Glorious and tragic in the sun and snow
And I know that one day I can go

Home